BOWLING ALLEY ADJECTIVES

By Doris Fisher and D. L. Gibbs
Cover illustrated by Scott Angle
Interior illustrated by Jeff Chandler
Curriculum consultant: Candia Bowles, M.Ed., M.S.

Gareth Stevens
Publishing

Please visit our web site at **www.garethstevens.com**.
For a free color catalog describing Gareth Stevens Publishing's list of high-quality books, call 1-800-542-2595 (USA) or 1-800-387-3178 (Canada). Gareth Stevens Publishing's fax: 1-877-542-2596

Library of Congress Cataloging-in-Publication Data

Fisher, Doris.
    Grammar all-stars / Doris Fisher and D. L. Gibbs.
      p. cm.
    ISBN-10: 0-8368-8901-0   ISBN-13: 978-0-8368-8901-7 (lib. bdg.)
    ISBN-10: 0-8368-8908-8   ISBN-13: 978-0-8368-8908-6 (pbk.)
    1. English language—Grammar—Juvenile literature. 2. English language—Parts of speech—Juvenile literature. 3. Sports—Juvenile literature. I. Gibbs, D.L. II. Title.
    PE1112.F538   2008
    428.2—dc22   2007033840

This edition first published in 2008 by
Gareth Stevens Publishing
A Weekly Reader® Company
1 Reader's Digest Road
Pleasantville, NY 10570-7000 USA

Copyright © 2008 by Gareth Stevens, Inc.

Senior Managing Editor: Lisa M. Guidone
Senior Editor: Barbara Bakowski
Creative Director: Lisa Donovan
Senior Designer: Keith Plechaty

Printed in the United States of America

2 3 4 5 6 7 8 9 10 09 08

CONTENTS

Look for the **boldface** words on each page.
Then read the **TENPIN TIP** that follows.

CHAPTER 1

THUNDER LANES

What Are Adjectives?

"Hi there, viewers!" says announcer Buzz Star. "Thanks for watching P-L-A-Y TV, the source for sports. I am coming to you from Thunder Lanes, where the strikes flash like lightning and the spares rumble! **This** match is the **final** game of the Tenpin Tournament. **Two** members of the Flower Power Bowling League are competing for the title. Lauren Lewis is with me for **this exciting** event. Lauren was the **best** speller at the bee held recently at Hillside School."

"**Which** word did you spell to win **that** title, Lauren?" asks Buzz.

"I spelled the word *adjective*," says Lauren.

"That's a **tricky** word to spell," says Buzz. "Did you have to know the definition, too?"

"Yes," says Lauren. "Adjectives are words that describe people, places, and things."

"Can you put **some** adjectives to work right now, Lauren? Describe for the viewers what's happening here at Thunder Lanes," says Buzz.

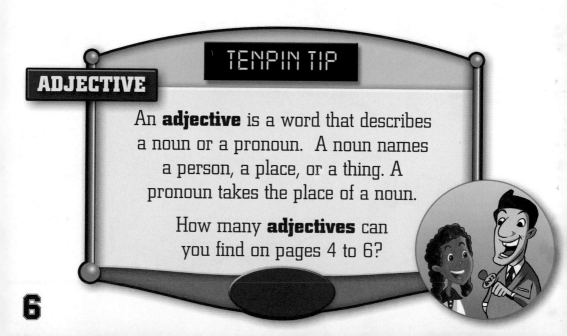

TENPIN TIP

ADJECTIVE

An **adjective** is a word that describes a noun or a pronoun. A noun names a person, a place, or a thing. A pronoun takes the place of a noun.

How many **adjectives** can you find on pages 4 to 6?

"Really, Mr. Star?" Lauren asks excitedly. "Can I really talk on TV?"

"You already are," Buzz says with a laugh. "Go ahead and tell everyone what you see."

"Sure," says Lauren, taking a **deep** breath.

"**This** alley is **huge**! I see **many** racks of **colorful** balls. The **wooden** lanes are **shiny**, with **long** gutters down **both** sides. **Ten white** pins are set up neatly at the end of **each** lane. The **four center** lanes are roped off for the **two** bowlers in the contest. The booth where I'm broadcasting is **nearby**, so I will have a **clear** view of the action. This match is **exciting**!"

"You did a **great** job, Lauren," says
Buzz. "Your report was very **descriptive**."

"Thank you," says Lauren, flashing a
big smile.

TENPIN TIP

ADJECTIVE

An **adjective** usually
comes before the noun it
describes—but not always.

Buzz speaks to the audience again. "Perry Winkle and Daisy Field are bowling in this contest, ladies and gentlemen. First they will roll some balls for practice. Then they will bowl for the cameras. Stay with us, folks, to see which of these two bowlers will take home the trophy!"

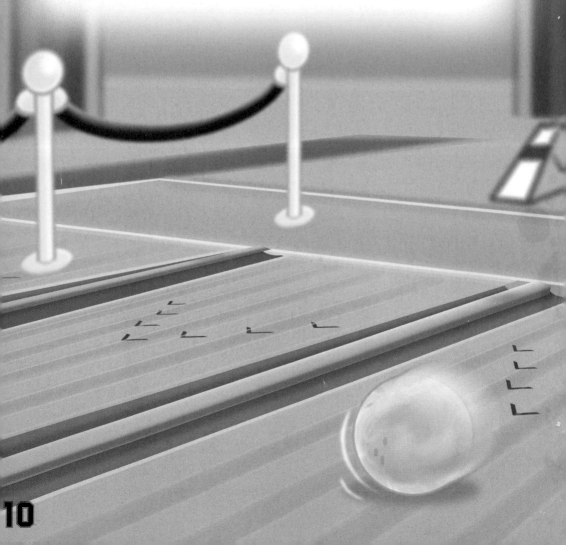

ALLEY ACTION

What Kind? Which One? How Many?

"Perry and Daisy are ready to roll," says Buzz. "Lauren, you do the reporting when Daisy is bowling. I'll describe the action when Perry bowls."

"I'm going to be a reporter!" says Lauren. "What should I say?"

"Just describe what you see," says Buzz. "Tell the viewers *what kind* of ball Daisy is using. Be sure to mention *which* lane she bowls on and *how many* pins she knocks down."

"Daisy is getting a ball, Lauren," Buzz adds. "You're on the air!"

"Um, hi, everybody! I'm Lauren Lewis. Daisy Field will bowl on the **left** lane. She is wearing **white** pants and a blouse with **pink** flowers on it. Daisy, a **left-handed** bowler, is holding a **bright yellow** ball. She is moving toward the lane … and there goes the ball. STRIKE! Daisy knocked down all of the pins. She looks **happy**. What a **great** start!"

TENPIN TIP

ADJECTIVE

An **adjective** can tell **what kind**.

Buzz takes over. "Perry Winkle is up next," he says. "All of the bowlers in the Flower Power Bowling League wear flowered clothing. **English** roses decorate the blouse Daisy has on. Perry is dressed in a **Hawaiian** shirt."

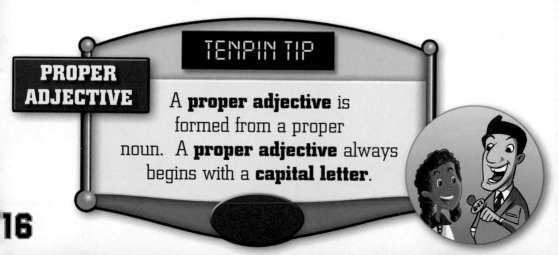

PROPER ADJECTIVE

TENPIN TIP

A **proper adjective** is formed from a proper noun. A **proper adjective** always begins with a **capital letter**.

"Look at all **those** flowered shirts!" says Lauren. "**That** group of people must be cheering for Perry and Daisy."

"**Those** fans are Flower Power Bowling League teammates," says Buzz. "They came to see **which** bowler will win **this** match."

TENPIN TIP

ADJECTIVE

An **adjective** can tell **which one** or **which ones**.

"Perry throws the ball, and it roars down the lane. It looks like a strike but … no! **Two** pins are standing. It's a split! If anyone can turn a split into a spare, Perry can. He comes from a **whole** family of bowlers. Perry takes a **second** throw. POW! The ball clobbers **one** pin and sends it sliding into the other for a spare. Wow! That was an exciting **first** frame. Stay with us, folks, for more action."

TENPIN TIP

ADJECTIVE

An **adjective** can tell **how much** or **how many**.

CHAPTER 3

STRIKES, SPARES, AND GUTTER BALLS

Comparisons

Buzz and Lauren take turns calling the action. The bowlers have played two games and eight frames in game three. They have rolled splits, spares, and strikes.

"Welcome back, viewers. This match has turned into a real nail-biter," says Buzz. "Daisy Field and Perry Winkle have won one game apiece in this three-game series. With only two frames left in the last game, we'll soon know who will take home the trophy."

"The crowd is **quiet**," says Lauren. "The fans become even **quieter** as each bowler takes a turn. It's the **quietest** crowd I have ever heard."

TENPIN TIP

COMPARE

An **adjective** can **compare** two or more people, places, or things.

"A gutter ball in the fifth frame really hurt Daisy," Buzz says. "She has a **lower** score. Daisy bowls next, though. Maybe she will be **luckier**."

"Daisy throws, and nine pins go down," Lauren says. "She rolls again and gets a spare. She needed a **higher** score to take the lead."

TENPIN TIP

COMPARE

Add **-er** to compare **two** people, places, or things.

FRAME 5

9 /

Perry rolls another strike. Now the bowlers will play the final frame.

"Daisy needs to bowl three strikes to stay alive," says Buzz. "This will be the **toughest** frame for her."

"Daisy looks calm as she picks up her ball," says Lauren. "She may be the **calmest** person in the building. She throws the ball and … it's a STRIKE! Daisy rolls again. A second strike! One more roll … STRIKE THREE! I'm glad we're not watching baseball! The fans are shouting the **loudest** cheers of the day."

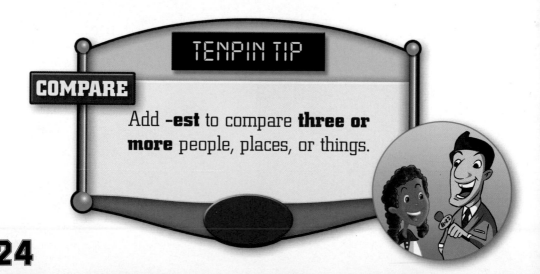

TENPIN TIP

COMPARE

Add **-est** to compare **three or more** people, places, or things.

FRAME 10

25

Buzz takes over as announcer. "Now Perry fires back with a strike. And there's another one! Perry needs one strike to win the championship. He rolls and … oh, no! It's a gutter ball!"

"Although Perry bowled **many** strikes, Daisy scored **more** points—the **most** points a bowler has ever scored in the Tenpin Tournament!" shouts Lauren.

"So, what do you think, Lauren?" asks Buzz.

"I think Perry and Daisy are **good** bowlers," says Lauren. "Daisy won, so I guess she was the **better** bowler today. She holds the title of **best** bowler in the city. But I think Perry is a winner, too."

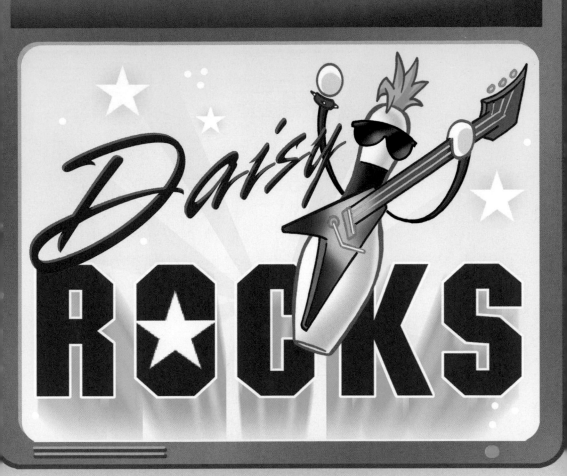

IRREGULAR ADJECTIVES

Irregular adjectives do not add **-er** or **-est** to form comparisons. They use special words that have to be memorized.

"Thank you for being my helper today," says Buzz. "You're a superstar speller and a great reporter."

"Thanks for letting me be on TV, Mr. Star," Lauren says. "It was fun. I mean, it was exciting. No, wait, it was thrilling!" She smiles. "You were right: I did use a lot of A-D-J-E-C-T-I-V-E-S."